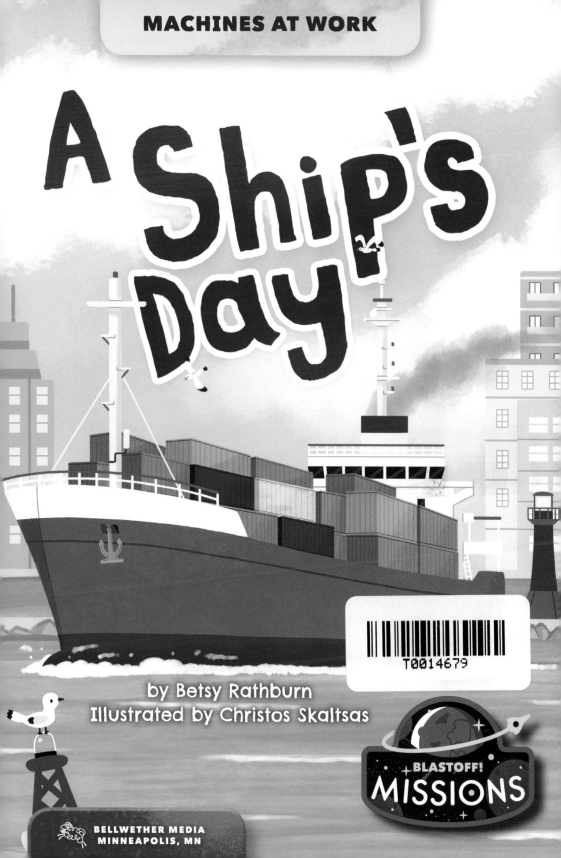

A Ship's Day

by Betsy Rathburn
Illustrated by Christos Skaltsas

BLASTOFF!
MISSIONS

BELLWETHER MEDIA
MINNEAPOLIS, MN

Blastoff! Missions takes you on a learning adventure! Colorful illustrations and exciting narratives highlight cool facts about our world and beyond. Read the mission goals and follow the narrative to gain knowledge, build reading skills, and have fun!

BLASTOFF!
MISSIONS

Traditional Nonfiction

BLASTOFF! READERS

BLASTOFF! Beginners

BLASTOFF! DISCOVERY

BLASTOFF! MISSIONS

Narrative Nonfiction

Blastoff! Universe

MISSION GOALS

> FIND YOUR SIGHT WORDS IN THE BOOK.

> LEARN ABOUT THE DAILY TASKS OF A CONTAINER SHIP.

> LEARN ABOUT DIFFERENT PARTS OF A CONTAINER SHIP.

This edition first published in 2024 by Bellwether Media, Inc.

No part of this publication may be reproduced in whole or in part without written permission of the publisher. For information regarding permission, write to Bellwether Media, Inc., Attention: Permissions Department, 6012 Blue Circle Drive, Minnetonka, MN 55343.

Library of Congress Cataloging-in-Publication Data

Names: Rathburn, Betsy, author.
Title: A ship's day / by Betsy Rathburn.
Description: Minneapolis, MN : Bellwether Media, Inc., 2024. | Series: Blastoff! Missions: Machines at work | Includes bibliographical references and index. | Audience: Ages 5-8 | Audience: Grades 2-3 | Summary: "Vibrant illustrations accompany information about the daily activities of a cargo ship. The narrative nonfiction text is intended for students in kindergarten through third grade."-- Provided by publisher.
Identifiers: LCCN 2023014284 (print) | LCCN 2023014285 (ebook) | ISBN 9798886873887 (library binding) | ISBN 9798886875263 (paperback) | ISBN 9798886875768 (ebook)
Subjects: LCSH: Cargo ships--Juvenile literature. | Marine terminals--Juvenile literature.
Classification: LCC HE566.F7 R37 2024 (print) | LCC HE566.F7 (ebook) | DDC 387.5/44--dc23/eng/20230428
LC record available at https://lccn.loc.gov/2023014284
LC ebook record available at https://lccn.loc.gov/2023014285

Editor: Christina Leaf   Designer: Andrea Schneider

Printed in the United States of America, North Mankato, MN.

This is **Blastoff Jimmy**! He is here to help you on your mission and share fun facts along the way!

Table of Contents

The sun rises over the ocean. The **container** ship has been waiting all night.

The **crew** lifts the ship's **anchor**. Time to move into the **port**!

container

port

crew

anchor

5

A **pilot** climbs aboard the ship. She meets the captain on the **bridge**.

She helps guide the ship into the port. Watch out for shallow areas!

pilot

PILOT

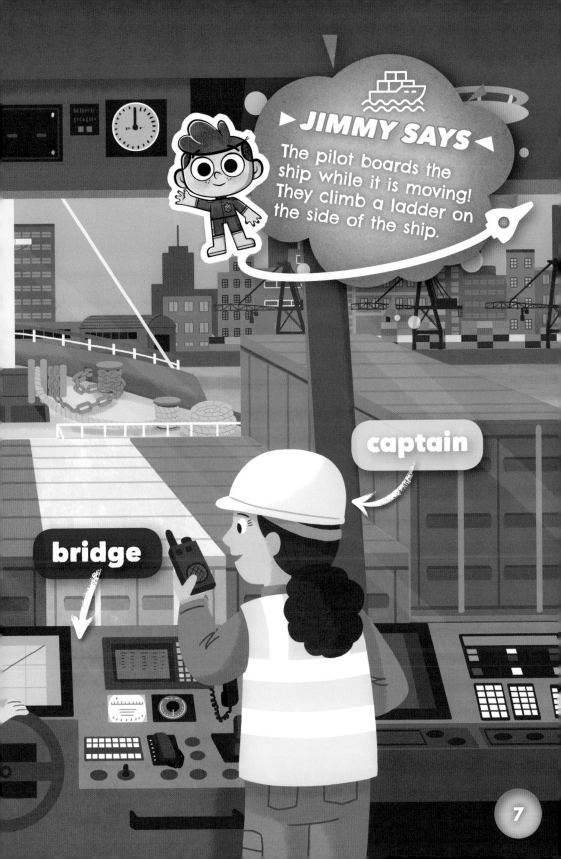

The ship needs help moving into the crowded port. It is hard to turn the huge ship!

Tugboats push and pull the ship into place.

tugboat

Containers and Cranes

deck

berth

All hands on **deck**! The crew works to **moor** the ship.

Heavy ropes hold it to the **berth**.

mooring the ship

crane

Next, the crew unhooks the stacked containers. A tall **crane** unloads them onto trucks.

JIMMY SAYS
The biggest container ships can hold more than 24,000 containers!

Special tools keep the ship from tipping to one side.

Finally, the containers are unloaded. It has taken the whole day!

The crew unties the ship from the berth. They get ready to set sail.

propellers

The pilot climbs aboard again. She helps the ship leave safely.

A horn blows as the ship exits the port. Giant **propellers** power the ship out to sea.

PILOT

The ship passes many other ships as it leaves the port.

That ship will carry fuel up a river. This one carries travelers!

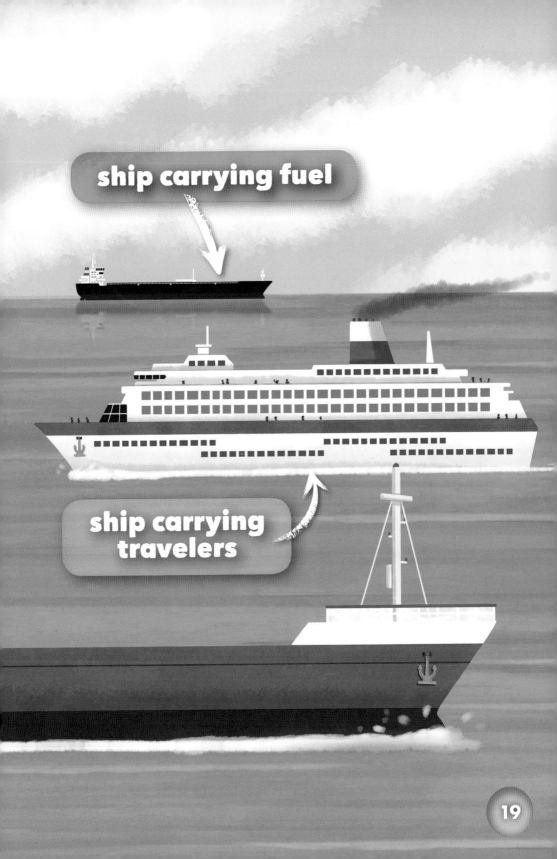

ship carrying fuel

ship carrying travelers

In a few days, the container ship will arrive at a new port. More containers will be loaded.

Then, the ship will cross the ocean again!

Ship Jobs

carry containers

carry fuel

carry travelers

Glossary

anchor–a heavy object attached to a chain that sinks to the seafloor and keeps a ship in place

berth–the place where a ship is tied up in a port

bridge–the part of a ship where people control the ship

container–a large metal box that holds goods to be shipped

crane–a machine with a long arm that lifts and moves heavy objects

crew–the people who work on a ship

deck–a flat surface of a ship where people can walk and where goods are stored

moor–to hold a ship in place using ropes or chains

pilot–a person who works in a port whose job is to help ships safely enter and exit the port

port–a place where ships load and unload their containers

propellers–parts of a ship that have blades that spin; propellers help a ship move through water.

tugboats–small, powerful boats that help ships move into place

To Learn More

AT THE LIBRARY

Gall, Chris. *Big Ship Rescue!* New York, N.Y.: Norton Young Readers, 2022.

Meister, Cari. *Boats and Ships.* North Mankato, Minn.: Capstone, 2019.

Rathbun, Betsy. *A Train's Day.* Minneapolis, Minn.: Bellwether Media, 2024.

ON THE WEB

FACTSURFER

Factsurfer.com gives you a safe, fun way to find more information.

1. Go to www.factsurfer.com.

2. Enter "ships" into the search box and click 🔍.

3. Select your book cover to see a list of related content.

BEYOND THE MISSION

> WHAT IS ONE FACT YOU LEARNED ABOUT CONTAINER SHIPS?

> WOULD YOU LIKE TO WORK ON A CONTAINER SHIP? WHY OR WHY NOT?

> IF YOU HAD A CONTAINER SHIP, WHAT WOULD IT CARRY?

Index